Why can't penguins fly?

Barbara Taylor

First published in 2011 by Miles Kelly Publishing Ltd
Harding's Barn, Bardfield End Green, Thaxted,
Essex, CM6 3PX, UK

2 4 6 8 10 9 7 5 3

Publishing Director Belinda Gallagher
Creative Director Jo Cowan
Editorial Director Rosie McGuire
Volume Designer Sally Lace
Cover Designer Kayleigh Allen
Image Manager Liberty Newton
Indexer Gill Lee
Production Manager Elizabeth Collins
Reprographics Stephan Davis
Assets Lorraine King, Cathy Miles

ISBN 978-1-84810-461-7

Printed in China

British Library Cataloguing-in-Publication Data

A catalogue record for this book is
available from the British Library

ACKNOWLEDGEMENTS
The publishers would like to thank the following
artist who has contributed to this book:

Mike Foster (character cartoons)

All other artwork from the Miles Kelly Artwork Bank

The publishers would like to thank the following
sources for the use of their photographs:

Corbis 26–27 Paul A. Souders
Fotolia.com 8–9 Grigory Kubatyan;
24 Fabrice Beauchene
digitalvision 11(l)
iStockphoto.com 11(r) Erlend Kvalsvik
Movie Store Collection 16–17 Warner Bros. Pictures,
Kingdom Feature Productions, Animal Logic,
Kennedy Miller Productions
Photolibrary.com 18–19 Gerard Lacz
Shutterstock.com 4–5 Eric Isselée; 8–9 Rich Lindie;
12–13 Steve Estvanik; 13 Karel Gallas; 17 Gentoo
Multimedia Ltd; 22 lfstewart; 29 Armin Rose

Every effort has been made to acknowledge the
source and copyright holder of each picture.
Miles Kelly Publishing apologises for any unintentional
errors or omissions.

Made with paper from a sustainable forest

www.mileskelly.net
info@mileskelly.net

www.factsforprojects.com

Self-publish your
children's book

buddingpress.co.uk

Contents

what is a penguin?

A penguin is a bird that spends most of its life in the ocean. It only comes onto land to lay eggs, look after its chicks and grow new feathers. Although penguins cannot fly, they are brilliant at swimming and diving.

Humboldt penguin

Are penguins the only flightless birds?

No, but most other flightless birds, such as ostriches and emus, live on land. They can run very fast to escape from enemies. The flightless cormorants of the Galapagos Islands are the only other seabirds that cannot fly.

Roly-poly penguin!

The name penguin may come from the Latin or Spanish word for fat! Penguins have lots of body fat to keep them warm.

Why can't penguins fly?

Penguins' wings are too short and stiff for flying. They are called flippers, and are a good size and shape for pushing the penguin along underwater. Penguins 'fly' underwater at about 8 kilometres an hour.

Royal penguin

Pretend

Can you move like a penguin? Hold your arms straight out at your sides and flap them up and down like flippers.

Is there only one kind of penguin?

No – there are 17 different species (kinds). They are mostly black and white, but the little penguin is blue and white. Some have black bands on their chests and heads. Others have bright crests or ear patches.

Magellanic penguin

Fjordland penguin

King penguin

Think
Look at the pictures of penguins in this book. Choose your favourite and make up your own name for it.

Do penguins like pasta?

No, but one type of penguin was named after the group of men who introduced macaroni pasta to England. The men wore feathers in their hats – a bit like the macaroni penguin's crest feathers.

Sports star!

Penguins don't need skis to get around in snow. They use their strong flippers to pull themselves uphill. To go downhill, they lie on their tummies and slide, like toboggans.

How big are penguins?

Different types of penguin are different sizes. The emperor penguin is the biggest and the little or fairy penguin is the smallest. The emperor is more than 20 times heavier than the little penguin, which weighs no more than a bag of sugar!

Little penguin is up to 45 centimetres tall

Emperor penguin is up to 1.15 metres tall

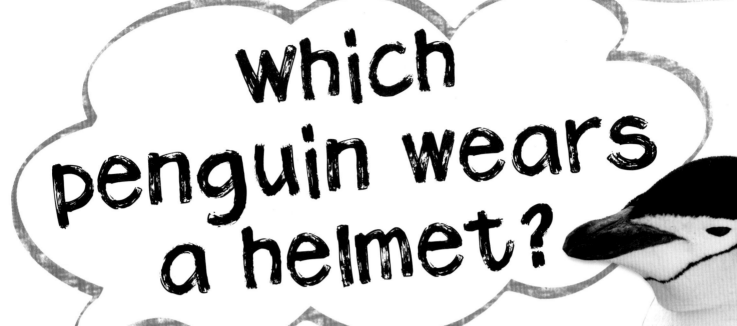

Which penguin wears a helmet?

The chinstrap penguin does! It has a band of black feathers that run from ear to ear under its bill. This makes it look as if it is wearing a helmet, with a strap under its chin.

Chinstrap penguin

Scary penguins!

An Adélie penguin will stare and point at rivals to keep them away from its nesting area. It may even beat other penguins with its flippers!

when is a penguin like a donkey?

When it's a jackass penguin! This penguin makes loud braying calls, which sound similar to the noises made by donkeys. Jackass penguins are also called African penguins because they live around the coasts of southern Africa.

Draw

Try drawing penguins with different hairstyles and haircuts. Choose a colour you like for the hair.

Snares penguin

why do some penguins have yellow hair?

Crested penguins have long yellow feathers above their eyes. This makes them look as if they have spiky yellow hair! Their colourful head crests help these penguins to recognize their friends and relatives and attract mates.

Are penguins tidy?

Adélie penguin

No – penguin nests are noisy, busy, messy places. But one group of penguins does have long tail feathers that sweep the ground as they walk. They are called brush-tailed penguins and include chinstrap penguins, Adélie penguins and gentoo penguins.

Shark surprise!

Like penguins, sharks are a dark colour on top and a light colour underneath. This helps them to sneak up on their prey in surprise attacks!

Why are most penguins black and white?

A penguin's colours help to camouflage (disguise) it from predators and prey. From above, its black back blends with the dark water below. From below, its white tummy blends with the light of the sky.

King penguin chick still with fluffy feathers

King penguin chick growing waterproof feathers

Do penguins mind getting wet?

Only when they are young. Penguin chicks have fluffy feathers at first, which are warm, but not waterproof. Chicks cannot go into the water until they have grown all their waterproof adult feathers.

Do polar bears live with penguins?

No – they never even meet! Penguins live in the southern half of the world and polar bears live in the north. Many kinds of penguins live in or around freezing Antarctica, but a few live in warmer places, such as Africa or New Zealand.

Adélie penguins

Do penguins get sunburnt?

Galapagos penguins live on the hot Galapagos Islands. Swimming in the ocean helps them to keep cool. On land, they hold their flippers over their feet to stop them getting sunburnt!

Penguin on ice!

Penguins have webbed feet with strong claws to stop them sliding on slippery ice. They hold their flippers out to help them balance when they waddle across ice and snow.

Discover

Look through this book and find one penguin that lives in a hot place and one penguin that lives in a cold place.

Jackass penguins

HOW do penguins keep cool?

Penguins that live in warmer places lose heat from patches of bare skin on their head, flippers and feet. They can also move into the shade or shelter in underground burrows to escape the hottest hours of day.

13

Why are penguins good swimmers?

Penguins have a smooth shape, so they move smoothly underwater. Their heavy bones help them to dive deep, and their long, flat flippers give power to their swimming strokes. Penguins use their tails and feet to steer and brake.

King penguins

Do leopards eat penguins?

No – but a spotted seal called a leopard seal does. These fast-swimming hunters have wide mouths and sharp teeth. They sneak up on penguins, carry them to the surface, and swallow them.

Leopard seal

Gentoo penguin

Sleepy penguins!

Penguins snooze at almost any time and can even take short naps while swimming! They mostly sleep at night and can fall asleep when they are standing or lying down.

Float

When you next go swimming, try floating. Take a deep breath, lie back and hold your arms and legs out in a star shape.

Can penguins hold their breath?

Yes, they hold their breath when they dive. Emperors can hold their breath for up to 18 minutes because they can store lots of oxygen inside their bodies. Little penguins can only hold their breath for about a minute.

Which penguin can tap-dance?

Mumble the emperor penguin, in the movie _Happy Feet_ can! In a world where every penguin needs a special song to attract a soulmate, poor Mumble has a terrible singing voice. Instead he has to tap-dance his way into the heart of the penguin he loves.

Think

Make up a story about a penguin who wants to star in a musical. Does his or her dream come true?

Mumble the tap-dancing penguin

16

Why do penguins go on long journeys?

Penguins nest on land but have to make long journeys back to the sea to collect food for their chicks. Parent Adélie penguins may travel up to 120 kilometres in search of food.

Bounce, bounce!

A penguin's layers of fat cushion its body from bumps when it moves over rocks. Its strong, leathery skin gives extra protection.

Rockhopper penguins

How fast can penguins walk?

Penguins can walk as fast as people. They look clumsy on land, but they can leap high out of the water onto ice and use their sharp claws and strong bills to pull themselves up rocks. Rockhopper penguins jump from rock to rock, which is how they got their name.

what do penguins eat?

Penguins are meat-eaters and catch their food in the sea. They eat mainly fish, squid and shrimp-like krill. Smaller penguins eat a lot of krill, which float on the surface of the sea at night. Larger penguins dive deeper and feed mainly on squid.

Big meal!

A penguin has no teeth, so it swallows its food whole. A sharp bill and spines on its tongue help the penguin to grip slippery, wriggly fish.

Humboldt penguin catching a fish

How do penguins feed their chicks?

Penguins cough up food to feed to their chicks. Parent birds hunt in the sea, storing food in their stomachs or in special pouches in their throats. Then they carry the food back to their hungry chicks.

Chinstrap penguin

Chicks

Can penguins catch food in the dark?

Some penguins catch their food deep down in the ocean where it is very dark. They have excellent eyesight and may also use their other senses, such as smell and hearing, to find food.

COUNT

See how many times you eat fish in a month. Fish is very good for you, especially oily fish such as sardines and tuna.

Are penguins show-offs?

Male penguins show off to impress females. They stretch up tall, point their bills towards the sky, beat their flippers and call loudly. Male chinstrap penguins put on a very noisy show — they sound like donkeys or hissing cats!

Chinstrap penguin displaying

How long can emperors go without food?

While keeping his egg warm, a male emperor penguin doesn't eat for more than 15 weeks. By the time his mate returns from her feeding trip out at sea, he may have lost up to half of his body weight.

Female

Male gentoo
with pebble

Build

Collect some pebbles from the beach, or some stones from the garden and build a stone nest for one of your toy animals.

when do penguins give presents?

When they are building a nest of pebbles, male Gentoo and Adélie penguins sometimes give their mates pebbles as presents. This helps make the nest bigger and shows that the males are serious about bringing up a family.

Take a bow!

A pair of Adélie penguins bow to each other when they meet. They also stretch upwards with bills open, calling loudly and swaying from side to side.

Why do penguins nest together?

So they can **huddle together for warmth, and so there are plenty of eyes to keep watch for predators.** In many of the places where penguins live, there is little space for nesting. A group of nesting penguins is called a rookery.

Gentoo penguin rookery

Royal penguins

when do penguins fight?

Penguins are irritable birds, often squabbling over nesting spaces and even stealing pebbles or other nesting materials from each other. They fight with their sharp beaks and strong flippers. Some fights are so fierce that eggs are crushed.

Discover
Find out how many penguins live together in a rookery. What is the biggest number you can discover?

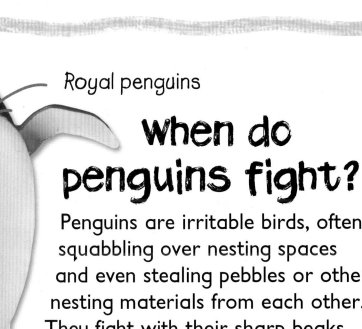

Fantastic fisherman!
Penguins are among only a few fish-eating animals that can survive in the freezing oceans around Antarctica. This means there is plenty of food for them to collect for their chicks!

How do penguins lose their eggs?

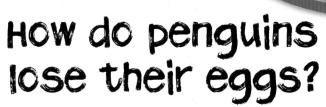

In hot weather, jackass penguins sometimes have to leave their nests to cool down in the sea. By the time they return, their eggs may have been eaten or stolen by seabirds.

Where do emperors keep their eggs?

When a female emperor penguin lays her egg, her mate puts it on top of his feet. He keeps it warm under a flap of skin – rather like a tea cosy. If the egg falls onto the ice, it will freeze and the chick inside will die.

Emperor penguins

Do penguins lay lots of eggs?

Emperor and king penguins only lay one egg but most other types of penguin lay two. The first chick to hatch often receives the most food, so it is more likely to survive than the second chick.

Make

Glue two small pieces of felt together to make an egg cosy for your boiled egg. Decorate your egg cosy with stickers, wool or ribbon.

Hungry chicks!

Penguin chicks may be tiny when they hatch, but they grow fast and are always hungry! Parent birds are kept busy finding enough food for them to eat.

Emperor penguin

How do penguins find their chicks?

Penguin parents can pick out the high-pitched calls of their own chicks amongst the noise of a busy rookery. Young chicks stretch up and beg for food, while older chicks peck at their parents' bills to make them cough up food.

Chicks

Which enemies eat eggs and chicks?

Hungry seabirds, such as gulls and skuas, lurk around the edge of penguin rookeries. They are always ready to take an easy meal of a penguin egg or chick. Parent penguins defend their eggs and chicks fiercely, and will not give them up without a fight.

Skua

King penguin

Draw

Sketch a picture of young penguins at a nursery school learning their letters, numbers and colours.

Egg

Nursery of emperor chicks

Do penguins go to school?

No, but their parents leave them in groups called nurseries. This happens when they are about seven weeks old. The chicks huddle together for warmth while their parents go off to sea to collect food for them.

Beware of the dog?

Dogs, cats, foxes and ferrets kill the chicks of yellow-eyed penguins. This species lives in New Zealand and is becoming rare.

Would a penguin peck a person?

Yes it would! Penguins are fierce birds and will attack people if they feel threatened. Thick jackets help to protect people from penguin bites.

which penguins are rare?

Galapagos penguin

Erect-crested penguin

About 11 penguin species are in danger of dying out completely (becoming extinct). These include the erect-crested penguin, the jackass penguin, the Galapagos penguin and the yellow-eyed penguin.

PENGUINS IN DANGER
- Emperor penguin
- King penguin
- Erect-crested penguin
- Galapagos penguin
- Gentoo penguin
- Chinstrap penguin
- Humboldt penguin
- Magellanic penguin
- Fjordland penguin
- Jackass penguin
- Rockhopper penguin

Emperor penguin

Hats off!

People used to hunt penguins. The skins were made into hats and purses, the fat was made into oil and the feathers were used to fill mattresses.

Are penguins in trouble?

Humans are not allowed to hunt penguins, but these birds are still in danger. Threats include not having enough food because people do too much fishing, pollution (rubbish) in the sea, and being hit by boats. Nesting places are also being destroyed, or disturbed by tourists.

Visit

Go to a zoo or an aquarium that keeps penguins, or watch a film about them. They are even more amazing in real life than they are in this book!

How much do we know about penguins?

Very little – especially about their lives while they are out at sea. The more we know, the easier it will be to protect them. Scientists have to be careful not to disturb penguins while they collect their data (information).

Quiz time

Do you remember what you have read about penguins? Here are some questions to test your memory. The pictures will help you. If you get stuck, read the pages again.

3. which penguin wears a helmet? | page 8

4. why are most penguins black and white? | page 11

5. Do polar bears live with penguins?

1. why can't penguins fly? | page 5

page 12

6. Do leopards eat penguins?

2. Do penguins like pasta? | page 7

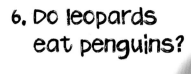

page 15

7. why do penguins go on long journeys?

8. How do penguins feed their chicks?

9. How long can emperors go without food?

10. why do penguins nest together?

11. How do penguins find their chicks?

12. would a penguin peck a person?

13. Are penguins in trouble?

Answers

1. Because their wings are too short and stiff for flying
2. No, but there is a type of penguin called the macaroni penguin
3. The chinstrap penguin's feathers make it look like it is wearing a helmet
4. To camouflage them from predators and prey
5. No – they never even meet
6. No, but leopard seals do
7. To collect food for their chicks
8. They store food in their throats or stomachs and cough it up for their chicks
9. More than 15 weeks
10. For warmth, and so there are lots of them to keep watch for predators
11. By listening for their high-pitched calls
12. Yes!
13. Yes – they are suffering from lack of food, pollution, being hit by boats, and the destruction of their nesting sites

Index